CCBMA Basic Exam: Practice Questions

First published in 2022

This edition was published on November 25, 2022

Visit Examelot's site at **examelot.com**

ISBN 9798442814309

CCBMA Basic Exam: Practice Questions

Examelot

Contents

About this book

This book is divided into two parts.

The first part of the book will go over the basics of the CCBMA Basic Exam and the topics the exam covers.

The second part of the book contains 300 questions, divided into the six sections of the exam. You can find the answers at the end of each section.

From the Examelot team, we wish you the best of luck in your CCBMA Basic Exam!

About the CCBMA Basic Exam

What is the CCBMA Basic Exam?

The California Certified Medical Assistant (CCMA) exams are exams that test your knowledge of medical assisting. They are designed for entry-level medical assistants.

The exams are set by the California Certifying Board for Medical Assistants (CCBMA), a private non-profit corporation.

There are three CCMA exams: Basic, Administrative and Clinical. The Basic exam tests your knowledge of fundamental principles of medical assisting, such as medical law, medical ethics, human anatomy and physiology, and medical terminology.

To become certified, you must pass:

1. the Basic examination and
2. either the Administrative exam or Clinical exam.

Eligibility requirements

To take the exam, you must be at least 18 years old and have CPR (cardiopulmonary resuscitation) certification. You must also meet one of the following requirements:

- Currently employed as a medical assistant in the United States
- Graduated from an accredited medical assisting program in the United States in the last year
- Have worked as a medical assistant in the United States for two years during the last five years

- Currently employed as a medical assisting instructor in the United States
- Member of the US military with relevant training

How to apply for the exam

You apply for the exam, you must apply online at the CCBMA website (ccbma.org). Upon approval of your application, CCBMA will send you an email with instructions on how to schedule your exam.

What's the exam like?

The exam takes place several times a year at testing centers across California. On your exam day, you'll need to go to your local Pearson VUE testing center. The staff there will check your identity document to confirm your identity. There will be a locker for you to keep your belongings. Then you'll be shown to a computer where you'll do the exam.

The Basic Exam is two hours long and consists of 175 multiple-choice questions. There are no breaks.

Don't bring calculators to the exam. Calculators will be provided on request at the testing center.

Passing the exam

Passing the exams gives you a CCBMA credential. There are three credentials you can receive:

- Passing the Basic and Administrative examinations gives you **a CCMA-A credential**.
- Passing the Basic and Clinical examinations gives you **a CCMA-C credential**.
- Passing the Basic, Administrative and Clinical examinations gives you **a CCMA-AC credential.**

What if I fail the exam?

If you fail the exam, you can retake it two more times. The retake fee is $105.

If you fail a third time, you can only retake the exam again if you work as a medical assistant. If you don't work as a medical assistant, then you'll no longer be able to retake the exam.

What if I need to cancel my exam?

To cancel your exam, you'll need to write to CCBMA at least 15 days before your exam date. You'll also need to contact Pearson VUE to have your scheduled appointment canceled. After you've canceled your exam, CCBMA will refund you the application fee minus a $50 processing charge.

What if I need to reschedule my exam?

To reschedule the exam, you'll need to contact Pearson VUE at the phone number found on your eligibility letter.

Structure of the exam

The CCMA Basic Exam has six sections:

- Section A: Medical terminology
- Section B: Technical references
- Section C: Structure and function of the human body
- Section D: Psychological aspects of medical assisting
- Section E: Legal and ethical issues
- Section F: Patient education

Sections A, B, and C are together worth 45% of the exam. Section D is worth 5%, Section E is worth 25% and Section F is worth 25%.

Section A: Medical Terminology

The first section of the Basic exam, *Medical Terminology*, includes the following topics:

- Definitions
- Word parts
- Abbreviations

Section B: Technical References

The second section of the exam, *Technical References*, includes the following topics:

- Medical and standard dictionaries
- PDR
- Diagnostic/procedural coding books

Section C: Structure and Function of the Human Body

The third section of the Basic exam, *Structure and Function of the Human Body*, will ask you questions about human anatomy and physiology. Topics in this section include:

- Organs
- Anatomical divisions
- Body planes
- Body positions and directions
- Body systems (integumentary, musculoskeletal, nervous, cardiovascular, respiratory, digestive, urinary, reproductive, endocrine, sensory)
- Correct spelling of terms

Section D: Psychological Aspects of Medical Assisting

The fourth section of the Basic exam, *Psychological Aspects of Medical Assisting*, is worth 5% of the exam and will include questions about:

- Communication skills
- Patient relations
- Professionalism

Section E: Legal and Ethical Issues

The fifth section of the exam, *Legal and Ethical Issues*, is worth 25% and will ask you questions about:

- Californian medical assistant regulations
- Californian medical practice law
- Drug enforcement administration regulations
- Consent
- Professional liability
- Medical records
- Confidentiality
- Patient rights
- Personal standards, hiring, and termination

Section F: Patient Education

The final section, *Patient Education*, is worth 25% of the exam and will ask you questions about:

- Instructions (written and oral)
- Prescriptions
- Diagnostic testing
- Nutrition
- Fitness

Practice questions

Section 1
Medical terminology

There are 62 questions in this section.

1.1 A forceful wrenching or twisting of a joint that tears or stretches its ligaments but does not dislocate the bones is called a:

(a) compression

(b) fracture

(c) sprain

(d) subluxation

1.2 What does the "F" stand for in FBS test?

(a) Fasting

(b) Fatal

(c) Final

(d) First

Answers on page 28

1.3 What is a meniscus?

(a) A type of balance

(b) The curved surface of a liquid

(c) The precipitate in a solution

(d) The tip of a pipette

1.4 A blood clot that forms in a vessel and remains there is called:

(a) a hematoma

(b) a thrombus

(c) an embolism

(d) an ischemia

1.5 What is a CCMSU?

(a) A blood test to diagnose cancer of the red blood cells

(b) A method of collecting urine samples

(c) A type of heart attack

(d) A type of x-ray

1.6 The final link in the chain of infection is someone at risk of infection. This person is called a __________ host.

(a) contagious

(b) reservoir

(c) resistant

(d) susceptible

Answers on page 28

1.7 Nosocomial infections are acquired in:

(a) homes

(b) hospitals

(c) nursing homes

(d) schools

1.8 Substances that prevent blood clotting are called:

(a) anticoagulants

(b) coagulants

(c) platelets

(d) thrombi

1.9 What does PSA stand for?

(a) Patient safety awareness

(b) Plasma-specific antibody

(c) Platelet-specific antigen

(d) Prostate-specific antigen

1.10 Small red or purple spots caused by a minor hemorrhage are called:

(a) palachiae

(b) parachiae

(c) pasachiae

(d) petechiae

Answers on page 28

1.11 ETS stands for ________ ________ system.

(a) electrical tube

(b) evacuated tube

(c) extravascular testing

(d) extravascular tube

1.12 BT and CT stand for:

(a) bile test and culture test

(b) bleeding time and clotting time

(c) blood test and clotting test

(d) blood tube and clot tube

1.13 What is edema?

(a) A bruise on the head

(b) A collection of blood outside blood vessels

(c) Swelling caused by fluid retention

(d) The final product of the blood coagulation step in hemostasis

1.14 What does ACD stand for?

(a) Acid citrate dextrose

(b) Acute calcium deficiency

(c) Advanced Crohn's disease

(d) Automated care defibrillator

Answers on page 28

1.15 Hemolysis is the destruction of which type of cell?

(a) Endothelial cells

(b) Platelets

(c) Red blood cells

(d) White blood cells

1.16 What is macrocytosis?

(a) A blood cancer

(b) A tumor

(c) Abnormally large red blood cells

(d) Too many white blood cells

1.17 What is thiamine?

(a) A respiratory stimulant

(b) A vitamin

(c) An amino acid

(d) An antibiotic

1.18 What does the term oliguria mean?

(a) A urine volume that is higher than normal

(b) A urine volume that is lower than normal

(c) The absence of urine

(d) The presence of crystals in the urine

Answers on page 29

1.19 The negative log of hydrogen ion concentration is better known as:

(a) SG

(b) pH

(c) pKa

(d) the T/S constant

1.20 What does the term P.C. mean?

(a) After 12 hours

(b) After consultation

(c) After exercise

(d) After meals

1.21 Urticaria is another name for:

(a) hives

(b) malignancy of the basal cells

(c) scales

(d) severe itching

1.22 Motor neurons are also called __________ neurons.

(a) afferent

(b) association

(c) efferent

(d) nervous

Answers on page 29

1.23 Neurons that carry impulses to the central nervous system are called ____________ neurons.

(a) brain

(b) mixed

(c) motor

(d) sensory

1.24 What is the medical term for the bones of the fingers?

(a) Carpals

(b) Patellas

(c) Phalanges

(d) Tarsals

1.25 Bone cells that absorb and remove unwanted bone tissue are called:

(a) calcani

(b) exocytes

(c) fossas

(d) osteoclasts

1.26 What is the medical term for the shoulder blade?

(a) Clavicle

(b) Patella

(c) Scapula

(d) Sternum

Answers on page 29

1.27 Which term means before meals?

(a) Antenatal

(b) Postpartum

(c) Postprandial

(d) Preprandial

1.28 Names of enzymes usually end with which suffix?

(a) -ase

(b) -cyte

(c) -osis

(d) -phage

1.29 Jaundice is the medical term for:

(a) inflamation

(b) skin disease

(c) the disease caused by the hepatitis A virus

(d) yellow skin

1.30 What is the medical term for fainting?

(a) Edema

(b) Exsanguination

(c) Syncope

(d) Vertigo

Answers on page 29

1.31 Coagulation is more commonly known as:

(a) clotting

(b) dissolving

(c) mixing

(d) sweating

1.32 What is the term for yellow discoloration of the skin due to high bilirubin levels?

(a) Cholestasis

(b) Hemolysis

(c) Jaundice

(d) Kernicterus

1.33 An iatrogenic illness is an illness that:

(a) has no obvious symptoms

(b) is caused by medical treatment

(c) is triggered by stress

(d) only occurs in old age

1.34 What is the medical term for an exaggerated feeling of well-being?

(a) Autism

(b) Euphoria

(c) Labile

(d) Paranoia

Answers on page 30

1.35 Adipose tissue is more commonly known as:

(a) bone

(b) cartilage

(c) fat

(d) skin

1.36 What does hypertrophy mean?

(a) Excess energy

(b) Increase in cell numbers

(c) Increase in size

(d) Underdeveloped

1.37 What term describes localized tumor growth?

(a) Anaplastic

(b) Carcinoma in situ

(c) Metastasis

(d) Pleomorphic

1.38 Which does the prefix adeno- refer to?

(a) Glands

(b) Joints

(c) Kidney

(d) Liver

Answers on page 30

1.39 What does the prefix epi- mean?

(a) Above

(b) Below

(c) Between

(d) Next to

1.40 Which suffix means falling, drooping, or prolapse?

(a) -pathy

(b) -plasty

(c) -ptosis

(d) -trophy

1.41 What does the suffix -emia refer to?

(a) Blood condition

(b) Enlargement

(c) Paralysis

(d) Surgical removal

1.42 The absence of pigment in the skin is called:

(a) albinism

(b) dermatitis

(c) melanism

(d) xanthoderma

Answers on page 30

1.43 Which prefix means skin?

(a) Adipo-

(b) Cutaneo-

(c) Ichthyo-

(d) Pachyo-

1.44 Which word means under a fingernail or toenail?

(a) Epidermis

(b) Hypoglossal

(c) Subcutaneous

(d) Subungual

1.45 What is an in vivo test?

(a) Experiments are performed in a laboratory

(b) Experiments are performed in a living organism

(c) Radionuclide is incorporated into a chemical substance

(d) Radiopharmaceuticals are used

1.46 What do diuretic medications do?

(a) Lower cholesterol

(b) Promote fluid excretion

(c) Stop blood clotting

(d) Widen blood vessels

Answers on page 30

1.47 The saclike membrane surrounding the heart is called the:

(a) bundle of His

(b) interatrial septum

(c) pericardium

(d) ventricle

1.48 Spongy, porous bone tissue is called:

(a) bone fissure

(b) bone sinus

(c) cancellous bone

(d) compact bone

1.49 A malignant tumor of smooth muscle is called:

(a) leiomyoma

(b) leiomyosarcoma

(c) rhabdomyoma

(d) rhabdomyosarcoma

1.50 What is melena?

(a) A complete absence of the pigment melanin

(b) A condition where the skin loses its pigment cells, causing patches in different areas of the body

(c) Black tarry stools

(d) Bleeding from the uterus

Answers on page 30

1.51 What is the space between nerve cells called?

(a) Subarachnoid space

(b) Subdural space

(c) Synapse

(d) Ventricle

1.52 What is the medical term for a bacterial infection of the middle ear?

(a) Barotitis

(b) Cholesteatoma

(c) Mastoiditis

(d) Otitis media

1.53 What is the medical term for indigestion?

(a) Aphagia

(b) Dyspepsia

(c) Dysphagia

(d) Polyphagia

1.54 What part of the body does the prefix phreno- refer to?

(a) Air sac

(b) Chest

(c) Diaphragm

(d) The membrane around the lungs

Answers on page 31

1.55 A high-pitched, wheezing sound caused by disrupted airflow is called:

(a) asthma

(b) diphtheria

(c) epistaxis

(d) stridor

1.56 What is hypercapnia?

(a) Decreased carbon dioxide in the blood

(b) High blood pressure

(c) High carbon dioxide levels in the blood

(d) Increased oxygen to the tissues

1.57 Hyperkalemia means high levels of which chemical element?

(a) Calcium

(b) Mercury

(c) Potassium

(d) Sodium

1.58 What is nephrolithotomy?

(a) Surgery to remove a bladder

(b) Surgery to remove a kidney

(c) Surgery to remove a kidney stone

(d) Surgery to remove cancerous tissue from a kidney

Answers on page 31

1.59 What does the word 'glomerular' refer to?

(a) A collecting chamber in the kidney

(b) A tube in the bladder

(c) A tube leading from the kidney to the bladder

(d) Small balls of capillaries in the kidney

1.60 What is the tube that leads from the epididymis to the urethra?

(a) Cowper duct

(b) Seminiferous tubule

(c) Ureter

(d) Vas deferens

1.61 What is the medical term for the foreskin of the penis?

(a) Glans penis

(b) Perineum

(c) Phimosis

(d) Prepuce

1.62 The absence of one of both testes is called:

(a) anorchism

(b) aspermia

(c) cryptorchism

(d) oligospermia

Answers on page 31

Answers on page 31

Answers for Section 1: Medical terminology

1.1 **c) sprain**

A fracture is a broken bone.

A subluxation is a partial dislocation within the body, typically in a joint.

1.2 **a) Fasting**

An FBS test is a fasting blood sugar test.

1.3 **b) The curved surface of a liquid**

A meniscus is a curve in the surface of a liquid when it touches another material.

1.4 **b) a thrombus**

A thrombus is a blood clot that forms in a vessel and remains there.

Thromboembolism is the wrong answer because this is a clot that travels to another location in the body.

1.5 **b) A method of collecting urine samples**

CCMSU is an abbreviation for clean-catch midstream urine.

1.6 **d) susceptible**

1.7 **b) hospitals**

1.8 **a) anticoagulants**

1.9 **d) Prostate-specific antigen**

Prostate-specific antigen (PSA) is an important marker for prostate cancer.

1.10 **d) petechiae**

1.11 **b) evacuated tube**

The evacuated tube system (ETS) is the standard equipment for venipuncture. It consists of a needle device, a tube holder, and an air-evacuated tube.

1.12 **b) bleeding time and clotting time**

Bleeding time (BT) and clotting time (CT) are tests used to detect occult hemostatic disorders.

1.13 **c) Swelling caused by fluid retention**

1.14 **a) Acid citrate dextrose**

1.15 **c) Red blood cells**

1.16 **c) Abnormally large red blood cells**

1.17 **b) A vitamin**

Thiamine is the chemical name for vitamin B1.

1.18 **b) A urine volume that is lower than normal**

Oliguria is a urine volume that is lower than normal.

Polyuria is a urine volume that is higher than normal.

Anuria is the absence of urine.

1.19 **b) pH**

pH is a measure of the relative amount of free hydrogen and hydroxyl ions.

1.20 **d) After meals**

P.C. is Latin for "post cibum" which means after meals.

1.21 **a) hives**

Urticaria is another name for hives (an itchy skin rash). Urticaria was named in the 18th century for its resemblance to the rash caused by a nettle of the genus Urtica. The word "urtica" is the Latin word for "nettle" and is also related to the Latin verb urere, meaning "to burn."

1.22 **c) efferent**

1.23 **d) sensory**

Sensory neurons carry impulses to the central nervous system.

Efferent, or motor, neurons transmit impulses from the central nervous system to effector organs such as muscles and glands.

1.24 **c) Phalanges**

1.25 **d) osteoclasts**

1.26 **c) Scapula**

The shoulder is made up of three bones: the scapula (shoulder blade), clavicle (collarbone) and humerus (upper arm bone).

1.27 **d) Preprandial**

1.28 **a) -ase**

Amylase, lipase and maltase are examples of enzymes ending in 'ase'.

1.29 **d) yellow skin**

1.30 **c) Syncope**

1.31 **a) clotting**

1.32 **c) Jaundice**

1.33 **b) is caused by medical treatment**

1.34 **b) Euphoria**

1.35 **c) fat**

1.36 **c) Increase in size**

1.37 **b) Carcinoma in situ**

1.38 **a) Glands**
'Adeno' refers to a gland or glands, as in adenoma and adenopathy.

1.39 **a) Above**
'Epi' means 'above', as in epidermis (the layer of skin above the other layers).

1.40 **c) -ptosis**

1.41 **a) Blood condition**
Words that end with -emia are blood conditions. Examples are leukemia (blood cancer), anemia (low levels of red blood cells), and uremia (the presence of urine waste products in the blood).

1.42 **a) albinism**

1.43 **b) Cutaneo-**
The prefix 'cutaneo' means skin. An example is subcutaneous, meaning under the skin.

1.44 **d) Subungual**

1.45 **b) Experiments are performed in a living organism**

1.46 **b) Promote fluid excretion**

1.47 **c) pericardium**

1.48 **c) cancellous bone**
Cancellous bone is the spongy tissue of mature adult bone.

1.49 **b) leiomyosarcoma**

1.50 **c) Black tarry stools**
Melena is black, tarry feces caused by bleeding in the upper gastrointestinal tract.

1.51 **c) Synapse**

1.52 **d) Otitis media**

1.53 **b) Dyspepsia**

1.54 **c) Diaphragm**
The prefix phreno- refers to the diaphragm (the muscle below the lungs).

1.55 **d) stridor**
Stridor is noisy breathing that occurs due to obstructed air flow through a narrowed airway.

1.56 **c) High carbon dioxide levels in the blood**

1.57 **c) Potassium**
Hyperkalemia (high potassium) is caused by too much potassium in the blood.

1.58 **c) Surgery to remove a kidney stone**
Nephrolithotomy is a procedure to remove kidney stones.

1.59 **d) Small balls of capillaries in the kidney**
The glomerulus is a network of capillaries at the beginning of each nephron in the kidney.

1.60 **d) Vas deferens**
The vas deferens, also called the sperm duct, is a tube that connects the epididymis and the urethra in men.

1.61 **d) Prepuce**

1.62 **a) anorchism**

Section 2
Technical References

There are 16 questions in this section.

2.1 Which of these statements about upcoding is false?

(a) Upcoding is a compliance risk

(b) Upcoding is considered health care fraud

(c) Upcoding is only an issue when it is intentional

(d) Upcoding is the act of using a higher level CPT code in a claim

2.2 What do CPT codes describe?

(a) Deaths

(b) Diagnoses

(c) Patients

(d) Procedures

Answers on page 38

2.3 The two-digit additions to CPT codes that describe extra details of a procedure are called:

(a) ICD-10 codes

(b) modifiers

(c) service codes

(d) supplemental codes

2.4 Which letter does HCPCS Level 2 use for diagnostic radiology services?

(a) D

(b) R

(c) S

(d) X

2.5 What is the code for a colostomy Infection?

(a) K61.0

(b) K82.2

(c) K90.3

(d) K94.02

2.6 CPT codes have how many digits?

(a) 3

(b) 4

(c) 5

(d) 6

Answers on page 38

2.7 The DSM is a guide for diagnosing:

(a) cancers

(b) heart attacks and strokes

(c) mental disorders

(d) skin problems

2.8 Current Procedural Terminology (CPT) is divided into how many categories of codes?

(a) 3

(b) 4

(c) 5

(d) 6

2.9 In metastatic osteosarcoma of the lung, the primary site is:

(a) bone

(b) connective tissue

(c) lung

(d) unknown

Answers on page 38

2.10 The ICPC has 3 axes. These are:

(a) reason for encounter, diagnosis and ability

(b) reason for encounter, diagnosis and action

(c) reason for visit, age and diagnosis

(d) reason for visit, diagnosis and ability

2.11 What do ICD codes represent?

(a) Diseases

(b) Hospital departments

(c) Insurance providers

(d) Procedures

2.12 A patient with an enlarged thyroid was taken to the OR where a frozen section biopsy was performed, followed by total thyroidectomy. You would code the:

(a) diagnostic procedure first followed by the therapeutic procedure

(b) diagnostic procedure only

(c) therapeutic procedure first followed by the diagnostic procedure

(d) therapeutic procedure only

2.13 The __________ is populated by 2 sources: a subset of the DAD data and data from the provinces that do not submit to CIHI

(a) CJRR

(b) HD

(c) HMDb

(d) HSMR

Answers on page 38

2.14 When a patient presents with burns which are described by the physician as "non healing" or "necrotic", code them as:

(a) complication of a burn

(b) current burn

(c) infection of a burn

(d) sequelae of a burn

2.15 The most responsible diagnosis:

(a) explains the reason for admission

(b) is based on the primary procedure

(c) reflects the diagnosis associated with greatest resources used

(d) replicates the primary diagnosis

2.16 Which medication is used as an ACE inhibitor for hypertension and heart failure?

(a) Atorvastatin

(b) Levothyroxine

(c) Lisinopril

(d) Metoprolol

Answers on page 38

Answers for Section 2: Technical References

2.1 **c) Upcoding is only an issue when it is intentional**
Upcoding - whether intentional or not - is a serious compliance risk that may lead to payer audits, reimbursement takebacks, and charges of abusive or fraudulent billing.

2.2 **d) Procedures**
CPT codes describe the procedures a patient has received.

2.3 **b) modifiers**
Modifiers are added to the end of a CPT code with a hyphen. They are used to provide extra details about a procedure.

2.4 **b) R**
An example is R0070, "Transportation of portable x-ray equipment and personnel to home or nursing home".

2.5 **d) K94.02**

2.6 **c) 5**
All CPT codes have five digits. For example, 10021 is the CPT node for fine-needle aspiration.

2.7 **c) mental disorders**
The DSM (Diagnostic and Statistical Manual of Mental Disorders) is a classification of mental disorders.

2.8 **a) 3**
There are three categories of CPT codes:
Category 1: Procedures and contemporary medical practices
Category 2: Clinical laboratory services
Category 3: Emerging technologies, services, and procedures

2.9 **a) bone**

2.10 **b) reason for encounter, diagnosis and action**

2.11 **a) Diseases**
The International Classification of Diseases (ICD) is a tool that assigns codes for diseases, symptoms, abnormal findings, circumstances, and external causes of diseases or injuries.

2.12 **d) therapeutic procedure only**

2.13 **c) HMDb**

2.14 **b) current burn**

2.15 **c) reflects the diagnosis associated with greatest resources used**

2.16 **c) Lisinopril**

Section 3

Structure and Function of the Human Body

There are 60 questions in this section.

3.1 What is the functional unit of the kidney?

(a) Glomerular tuft

(b) Glomerulus

(c) Loop of Henle

(d) Nephron

3.2 Respiratory acidosis is a condition where:

(a) acid has entered a person's lungs

(b) the blood is too acidic

(c) the lungs cannot remove enough carbon dioxide from the body

(d) the pH of tissue is higher than the normal range

Answers on page 56

3.3 Which gland secretes cortisol?

(a) Adrenal cortex

(b) Adrenal medulla

(c) Pituitary gland

(d) Testes

3.4 Insulin is a:

(a) autocrine

(b) circulating hormone

(c) local hormone

(d) neurotransmitter

3.5 Which term means away from the origin?

(a) Anterior

(b) Distal

(c) Lateral

(d) Posterior

3.6 Substances travel from the glomerulus into the Bowman capsule by the process of:

(a) active transport

(b) diffusion

(c) filtration

(d) osmosis

Answers on page 56

3.7 Meiosis:

(a) consists of only one stage of cell division, not two

(b) happens in somatic cells

(c) involves the crossing over of genetic material

(d) is how the body grows and replaces worn-out cells

3.8 Which hormone directly regulates blood glucose levels?

(a) FSH

(b) Insulin

(c) Progesterone

(d) TSH

3.9 Cortisol levels are generally highest at:

(a) 8 am

(b) 12 pm

(c) 4 pm

(d) 8 pm

3.10 Which part of the brain regulates muscle tone and coordination?

(a) Cerebellum

(b) Frontal lobes

(c) Hypothalamus

(d) Medulla

Answers on page 56

3.11 During exercise, blood flow within a muscle is increased by:

(a) homogenization

(b) hyalinization

(c) precipitation

(d) vasodilatation

3.12 The function of the respiratory system is to:

(a) make enzymes

(b) regulate the endocrine system

(c) regulate the heartbeat

(d) supply oxygen to tissue and remove carbon dioxide from tissue

3.13 Which monosaccharide is the main end product of carbohydrate digestion?

(a) Glucose

(b) Lactose

(c) Maltose

(d) Sucrose

3.14 Which enzyme breaks down protein in the stomach?

(a) Amylase

(b) Lipase

(c) Pepsin

(d) Trypsin

Answers on page 56

3.15 Muscles are attached to bones by:

(a) blood vessels

(b) fascia

(c) other muscles

(d) tendons

3.16 Blood passing through the left atrium next enters the:

(a) aorta

(b) left lung

(c) left ventricle

(d) right atrium

3.17 What color is bilirubin?

(a) Blue

(b) Red

(c) White

(d) Yellow

3.18 Bright red blood in stools is usually caused by bleeding in the:

(a) higher intestinal tract

(b) lower gastrointestinal tract

(c) small intestine

(d) stomach

Answers on page 57

3.19 What is the function of the medulla?

(a) Control voluntary actions in the body

(b) Mediate visual and auditory reflexes

(c) Regulate heartbeat and respiration

(d) Store memory

3.20 The brain is located in which cavity?

(a) Abdominal

(b) Cranial

(c) Pericardial

(d) Pleural

3.21 Which term means nearer to the sacral (lowermost) region of the spinal cord?

(a) Caudal

(b) Distal

(c) Horizontal

(d) Lateral

3.22 Blood returning from the lungs first enters which part of the heart?

(a) left atrium

(b) left ventricle

(c) right atrium

(d) right ventricle

Answers on page 57

3.23 The small intestine consists of the duodenum, jejunum and:

(a) cecum

(b) colon

(c) ileum

(d) rectum

3.24 Which part of the brain regulates heart rate and blood pressure?

(a) Cerebellum

(b) Frontal lobe

(c) Hypothalamus

(d) Medulla

3.25 Which gland produces melatonin?

(a) Hypothalamus

(b) Pancreas

(c) Pineal gland

(d) Thymus

3.26 Antidiuretic hormone (ADH) stimulates the re-absorption of:

(a) hydrogen ions

(b) oxygen

(c) potassium

(d) water

Answers on page 57

3.27 Which hormone is also known as epinephrine?

(a) Adrenaline

(b) Cortisol

(c) Testosterone

(d) Vasopressin

3.28 Nerve cells are also called:

(a) axons

(b) glial cells

(c) neuroglial cells

(d) neurons

3.29 Neurons that transmit nerve impulses toward the central nervous system are called:

(a) bipolar neurons

(b) interneurons

(c) motor neurons

(d) sensory neurons

3.30 What are the end products of protein digestion?

(a) Amino acids

(b) Fatty acids

(c) Monosaccharides

(d) Triglycerides

Answers on page 57

3.31 When a muscle contracts, it:

(a) lengthens and pulls a bone

(b) lengthens and pushes a bone

(c) shortens and pulls a bone

(d) shortens and pushes a bone

3.32 The smallest blood vessels are called:

(a) arteries

(b) capillaries

(c) lymph vessels

(d) veins

3.33 Which of these is not part of the large intestine?

(a) Anal canal

(b) Cecum

(c) Duodenum

(d) Rectum

3.34 The somatic nervous system is also called the __________ nervous system.

(a) parasympathetic

(b) peripheral

(c) sympathetic

(d) voluntary

Answers on page 58

3.35 What is the motile tail of sperm called?

(a) Flagellum

(b) Microtubule

(c) Microvillus

(d) Nucleus

3.36 Which term means a location towards the front?

(a) Anterior

(b) Distal

(c) Lateral

(d) Posterior

3.37 What gives urine its yellow color?

(a) Urea

(b) Uric acid

(c) Urobilin

(d) Urobilinogen

3.38 Which muscles are the triangular muscles of the shoulder?

(a) Biceps

(b) Deltoids

(c) Long abductors

(d) Triceps

Answers on page 58

3.39 When calcium levels are low, the body produces:

(a) parathyroid hormone

(b) calcitonin

(c) epinephrine

(d) corticotropin

3.40 Which of these hormones is produced by the pituitary gland?

(a) Insulin

(b) T4

(c) TRH

(d) TSH

3.41 Neuron axons are electrically insulated by:

(a) astrocytes

(b) gray matter

(c) myelin sheaths

(d) white matter

3.42 The largest vein in the body is the:

(a) aorta

(b) hepatic portal vein

(c) pulmonary vein

(d) vena cava

Answers on page 58

3.43 Which system transports oxygen to muscles?

(a) Circulatory

(b) Lymphatic

(c) Respiratory

(d) Skeletal

3.44 The sequence of blood cell development in the embryo and fetus is:

(a) bone marrow, liver/spleen, yolk sac

(b) liver/spleen, yolk sac, bone marrow

(c) yolk sac, bone marrow, liver/spleen

(d) yolk sac, liver/spleen, bone marrow

3.45 Which of these fluids is associated with the lungs?

(a) Gastric

(b) Peritoneal

(c) Pleural

(d) Synovial

3.46 Which of these is a cord of connective tissue that connects a muscle to a bone?

(a) Cartilage

(b) Ligament

(c) Muscle fiber

(d) Tendon

Answers on page 59

3.47 Which anterior pituitary hormone stimulates milk production?

(a) Adrenocorticotropic hormone

(b) Luteinizing hormone

(c) Melanocyte stimulating hormone

(d) Prolactin

3.48 Which gland produces thyroid-stimulating hormone?

(a) Parathyroids

(b) Pituitary

(c) Testes

(d) Thyroid

3.49 The impulse in a neuron moves:

(a) from the Schwann cell to the myelin

(b) from the axon to the dendrite

(c) from the cell body to the myelin

(d) from the dendrite to the axon

3.50 Which of these is an organ of the endocrine system?

(a) Brain

(b) Pancreas

(c) Spleen

(d) Stomach

Answers on page 59

3.51 What are the three types of muscle tissue?

(a) Cardiac, smooth, and skeletal

(b) Internal, external and connectors

(c) Peripheral, central and core

(d) Protractors, retractors and reactors

3.52 The central nervous system includes the:

(a) brain and spinal cord

(b) heart

(c) somatic nerves

(d) spinal nerves

3.53 The axon terminal of a motor neuron releases:

(a) acetylcholine

(b) chlorine ions

(c) cholinesterase

(d) sodium ions

3.54 The part of a neuron that carries impulses away from the cell body is the:

(a) axon

(b) cell body

(c) dendrite

(d) myelin sheath

Answers on page 59

3.55 Which hormone controls sodium reabsorption?

(a) Aldosterone

(b) Angiotensin II

(c) Anti-diuretic Hormone

(d) Renin

3.56 What is the term for movement away from the midline of the body?

(a) Abduction

(b) Adduction

(c) Inversion

(d) Retrusion

3.57 Which skin structure helps prevent water loss and inhibits bacterial growth on the surface of the skin?

(a) Arrector pili

(b) Hair follicles

(c) Oil glands

(d) Sweat glands

3.58 Thyroid-stimulating hormone is also known as:

(a) thyroglobulin

(b) thyrotropin

(c) thyroxine

(d) triiodothyronine

Answers on page 59

3.59 The parasympathetic nervous system:

(a) decreases the metabolic rate

(b) is also known as the enteric nervous system

(c) is part of the somatic nervous system

(d) is under voluntary control

3.60 Which of these hormones is produced by the adrenal cortex?

(a) Cortisol

(b) Epinephrine

(c) Insulin

(d) Norepinephrine

Answers on page 60

Answers for Section 3: Structure and Function of the Human Body

3.1 **d) Nephron**

3.2 **c) the lungs cannot remove enough carbon dioxide from the body**

Respiratory acidosis is a condition that occurs when the lungs cannot remove all of the carbon dioxide the body produces. This causes body fluids, especially the blood, to become too acidic.

3.3 **a) Adrenal cortex**

3.4 **b) circulating hormone**

Insulin is an example of a circulating hormone (a hormone that is released by a gland and then carried in the bloodstream to distant target cells).

3.5 **b) Distal**

3.6 **c) filtration**

3.7 **c) involves the crossing over of genetic material**

3.8 **b) Insulin**

3.9 **a) 8 am**

In most people, cortisol levels are highest in the morning when they wake up. Cortisol levels are typically lowest around midnight.

3.10 **a) Cerebellum**

3.11 **d) vasodilatation**

Vasodilation is the dilatation of blood vessels.

3.12 **d) supply oxygen to tissue and remove carbon dioxide from tissue**

3.13 **a) Glucose**

The end product of carbohydrate digestion is mainly glucose.

3.14 **c) Pepsin**

Pepsin breaks down proteins into smaller peptides.

Amylase breaks down starches into maltose.

Lipase breaks down fats.

Trypsin, like pepsin, breaks down protein, but trypsin is found in the intestine instead of the stomach.

3.15 **d) tendons**

3.16 **c) left ventricle**

3.17 **d) Yellow**

3.18 **b) lower gastrointestinal tract**

When blood in the stool is bright red, the site of bleeding is most likely from the lower gastrointestinal tract.

3.19 **c) Regulate heartbeat and respiration**

The medulla is a long stem-like structure that makes up the lower part of the brainstem. It is sometimes called the medulla oblongata. It contains the cardiac, respiratory, vomiting and vasomotor centres and deals with the autonomic functions of breathing, heart rate and blood pressure.

3.20 **b) Cranial**

3.21 **a) Caudal**

3.22 **a) left atrium**

3.23 **c) ileum**

The small intestine consists of the duodenum, jejunum, and ileum.

The large intestine consists of the cecum, colon, rectum, and anal canal.

3.24 **d) Medulla**

The medulla is responsible for important bodily functions such as heartbeat and breathing, It is found in the brainstem.

3.25 **c) Pineal gland**

3.26 **d) water**

ADH signals the kidneys to conserve water and produce less urine.

3.27 **a) Adrenaline**

3.28 **d) neurons**

3.29 **d) sensory neurons**

3.30 **a) Amino acids**

3.31 **c) shortens and pulls a bone**

3.32 **b) capillaries**

3.33 **c) Duodenum**

The large intestine comprises the caecum, colon, rectum, anal canal and anus.
The duodenum is part of the small intestine.

3.34 **d) voluntary**

The somatic nervous system is associated with activities that are conscious or voluntary, such as walking and eating.

3.35 **a) Flagellum**

The flagellum allows the sperm to move by creating a whip-like motion.

3.36 **a) Anterior**

3.37 **c) Urobilin**

The yellow color of urine is caused by urobilin, a waste product generated from the breakdown of old red blood cells.

Urobilinogen is the wrong answer as it is colorless.

3.38 **b) Deltoids**

3.39 **a) parathyroid hormone**

When the body's calcium levels are low, parathyroid hormone stimulates the release of calcium from the bones to the bloodstream.

Calcitonin has the opposite effect by reducing calcium levels that are too high.

3.40 **d) TSH**

Insulin is incorrect as it is produced by the pancreas.

T4 is incorrect as it is produced by the thyroid gland.

TRH (thyrotropin-releasing hormone) is incorrect as it is produced by the hypothalamus.

3.41 **c) myelin sheaths**

Like the insulation around the wires in electrical systems, glial cells form a membraneous sheath surrounding axons called a myelin sheath, thereby insulating the axon.

3.42 **d) vena cava**

3.43 **a) Circulatory**

3.44 **d) yolk sac, liver/spleen, bone marrow**

3.45 **c) Pleural**

3.46 **d) Tendon**

Tendons connect muscle to bone.

Ligaments connect bone to bone.

Cartilage is a tissue that protects the ends of bones at the joints.

Muscle fiber is what muscles are made up of.

3.47 **d) Prolactin**

3.48 **b) Pituitary**

Thyroid-stimulating hormone (TSH) is produced by the pituitary gland. It stimulates the thyroid gland to produce T3 and T4.

3.49 **d) from the dendrite to the axon**

3.50 **b) Pancreas**

The endocrine system is a series of glands that produce and secrete hormones. The major glands of the endocrine system are the pineal gland, pituitary gland, pancreas, ovaries, testes, thyroid gland, parathyroid gland, hypothalamus and adrenal glands.

"Brain" is incorrect because it is part of the nervous system.

"Spleen" is incorrect because it is part of the lymphatic system.

"Stomach" is incorrect because it is part of the digestive system.

3.51 **a) Cardiac, smooth, and skeletal**

3.52 **a) brain and spinal cord**

3.53 **a) acetylcholine**

3.54 **a) axon**

3.55 **a) Aldosterone**

Aldosterone keeps sodium in the body and releases potassium from the body.

3.56 **a) Abduction**

A movement of a body part away from the midline is termed abduction. A movement of the body part back toward the midline is known as adduction.

3.57 **c) Oil glands**

3.58 **b) thyrotropin**

Thyroid stimulating hormone is also known as thyrotropin or thyrotrophin.

3.59 **a) decreases the metabolic rate**

The parasympathetic nervous system decreases respiration and heart rate and increases digestion.

3.60 **a) Cortisol**

Of the options, only cortisol is made in the adrenal cortex.

Epinephrine is made in the adrenal medulla.

Insulin is made by the pancreas.

Norepinephrine is made in the adrenal medulla.

Section 4

Psychological Aspects of Medical Assisting

There are 15 questions in this section.

4.1 A patient is extremely anxious about having her blood drawn. She tells you that she is afraid of needles. You do not have much experience drawing blood. What should you do?

(a) Ask an experienced phlebotomist to perform the draw for you

(b) Explain to her that you will use a small needle that barely hurts

(c) Tell her that it's not a big deal and that she shouldn't be afraid

(d) Use an ice pack to numb the site before drawing the specimen

4.2 How large is letter size paper?

(a) 5 by 8 inches

(b) 8.5 by 11 inches

(c) 11 by 17 inches

(d) 17 by 22 inches

Answers on page 66

4.3 Another word for compassion is:

(a) generosity

(b) greed

(c) selfishness

(d) sympathy

4.4 Pronouncing words clearly is called:

(a) emphasis

(b) enunciation

(c) intonation

(d) modulation

4.5 A young woman comes to get her blood drawn. She looks nervous. She says this is her first venipuncture. You should:

(a) carefully explain the procedure to her

(b) give her a stick to bite down on

(c) ignore her nervousness

(d) tell her she is too old to be scared

4.6 What is deportment?

(a) the failure to do the right thing

(b) the interference of a worker's personal life with their job

(c) the way a person behaves and presents themselves

(d) unprofessional behavior at work

Answers on page 66

4.7 Which of the following is proper telephone technique?

(a) Be careful of your tone of voice used and keep answers simple

(b) Do not identify yourself in case there are problems later

(c) Do not take notes because it takes too much time

(d) Wait for the phone to ring three or four times so as not to appear anxious

4.8 What is the most common letter style used in medical offices?

(a) Full-block

(b) Modified-block

(c) Modified-block with indented paragraphs

(d) Simplified

4.9 When answering the phone, you should say your name and:

(a) "How are you today?"

(b) the name of your facility

(c) your facility's opening hours

(d) your phone number

4.10 Which of these is proper telephone etiquette?

(a) Hanging up if the caller is annoying you

(b) Introducing yourself immediately upon picking up the phone

(c) Leaving the caller on hold for a long time

(d) Multi-tasking while listening to the caller

Answers on page 66

4.11 Which of these is the correct dateline for a business letter?

(a) 8/20/2015

(b) Aug. 20 2015

(c) Aug. 20, 2015

(d) August 20, 2015

4.12 In a business letter, the "inside address" is:

(a) the courier's address

(b) the receiver's address

(c) the return address

(d) the sender's address

4.13 The knowledge, skill, ability, or characteristic associated with high performance on a job, such as problem-solving, analytical thinking, or leadership is known:

(a) competency

(b) human resource training

(c) performance development

(d) work ethic

Answers on page 66

4.14 In formal business letters, which punctuation mark should follow the salutation?

(a) Colon

(b) Comma

(c) Period

(d) Semicolon

4.15 The obligation to act in a competent manner according to the standards of practice is:

(a) autonomy

(b) duty of care

(c) nonmaleficence

(d) the Good Samaritan law

Answers on page 66

Answers for Section 4: Psychological Aspects of Medical Assisting

4.1 **a) Ask an experienced phlebotomist to perform the draw for you**

4.2 **b) 8.5 by 11 inches**

4.3 **d) sympathy**
Some common synonyms of compassion are commiseration, condolence, pity, and sympathy.

4.4 **b) enunciation**

4.5 **a) carefully explain the procedure to her**
As this patient has never had venipuncture before, it may help to reassure her if you explain the procedure to her.

4.6 **c) the way a person behaves and presents themselves**

4.7 **a) Be careful of your tone of voice used and keep answers simple**

4.8 **a) Full-block**

4.9 **b) the name of your facility**

4.10 **b) Introducing yourself immediately upon picking up the phone**
You should always introduce yourself when picking up the phone so the caller knows she is talking to the right person.

4.11 **d) August 20, 2015**
The dateline should contain the month (fully spelled out), day, and year.

4.12 **b) the receiver's address**
The inside address in business letters is the address of the recipient you are sending your letter to.

4.13 **a) competency**

4.14 **a) Colon**
In business letters, the salutation is followed by a colon (e.g. Dear Mr. Smith:).
In personal letters, the salutation is followed by a comma (e.g. Dear Mr. Smith,).

4.15 **b) duty of care**

Section 5
Legal and Ethical Issues

There are 72 questions in this section.

5.1 What is the term for the mechanisms and processes designed to protect health information from unauthorized access?

(a) Accountability

(b) Confidentiality

(c) Privacy

(d) Security

5.2 In California, laboratories must report an acute HIV infection to the local health officer within one:

(a) hour

(b) working day

(c) week

(d) month

Answers on page 90

5.3 The release of a medical record without a patient's permission is:

(a) acceptable as long as the doctor signs off on it

(b) acceptable in most medical institutions

(c) an example of assault and battery

(d) an invasion of privacy

5.4 In HIPAA, PHI stands for __________ health information.

(a) patient

(b) personal

(c) private

(d) protected

5.5 The process for getting permission before conducting a healthcare intervention on a person is called:

(a) competency

(b) decision capacity

(c) informed consent

(d) risk management

5.6 __________ is the obligation of a lab assistant to not disclose health information unless authorized by law or the patient.

(a) Accountability

(b) Confidentiality

(c) Privacy

(d) Security

Answers on page 90

5.7 Law originating from court decisions is known as:

(a) common law

(b) public law

(c) statute law

(d) tort law

5.8 In which of these circumstances does a person's consent to have their information shared NOT need to be obtained?

(a) A media request

(b) A public health occurrence

(c) A request by family

(d) Facility fundraising

5.9 if a patient becomes unable to handle his own health care decisions, which document allows a proxy to handle the decisions for him?

(a) DNR orders

(b) Living will

(c) Medical power of attorney

(d) Organ donation

Answers on page 90

5.10 A failure to act reasonably and carefully, resulting in injury or harm to another person, is called:

(a) divine right

(b) negligence

(c) restitution

(d) rule of law

5.11 A term that means 'being held responsible' is:

(a) accountability

(b) communication

(c) competence

(d) safety

5.12 You have to draw your friend's blood. You notice that two of the tests ordered are Hepatitis and HIV. His girlfriend does not know about these tests. You should:

(a) say nothing to his girlfriend

(b) tell his girlfriend about the tests

(c) warn his girlfriend that he might have Hepatitis or AIDS

(d) warn his girlfriend that you think he is cheating on her

Answers on page 90

5.13 In California, in which situation can a pharmacist fill a prescription written by an unlicensed person?

(a) When the patient has an infectious disease

(b) When the pharmacy is in the hospital where the unlicensed person works

(c) When the prescription is signed by the patient's nurse

(d) When the prescrption contains the name and address of a licensed person

5.14 California is an "at-will" state. This means:

(a) patients have the right to leave the hospital, even if the healthcare provider thinks they should stay

(b) terminally-ill adults can request a drug to end their life

(c) users must take deliberate action to agree to terms and conditions

(d) workers can quit or be fired for any reason, as long as the reason is not illegal

5.15 How many people is considered a foodborne illness outbreak?

(a) 1

(b) 2

(c) 5

(d) 10

5.16 Which type of law enforces legally-binding agreements between two parties?

(a) Contract law

(b) Corporate law

(c) Criminal law

(d) Statute law

Answers on page 90

5.17 In California, can discovery continue after a case has been assigned to arbitration?

(a) Yes, until the day of the hearing

(b) Yes, until 3 days before the hearing

(c) Yes, until 15 days before the hearing

(d) No, once a case is assigned to arbitration discovery must stop

5.18 The process whereby an individual is informed of and agrees to the collection, use and disclosure of personal information is called:

(a) accountability

(b) consent

(c) openness

(d) safeguarding

5.19 Which of these actions helps to ensure patient confidentiality?

(a) Discarding old records by throwing them into the trash

(b) Giving out patient information to journalists

(c) Sending confidential material via e-mail

(d) Verifying the phone number of the receiving location before faxing confidential material

Answers on page 91

5.20 Patient personal information:

(a) may be discussed during coffee breaks

(b) may be discussed with other patients

(c) may be used for your personal advantage

(d) must never be discussed outside the hospital

5.21 A lawyer asks a lab technician for copies of his client's test results. What should the lab technician do?

(a) Ask the lawyer to submit his request in writing

(b) Give the results to the lawyer

(c) Have the lawyer sign a Medical Release Form before releasing the results

(d) Tell the lawyer that the laboratory can only release information to the physician who ordered the tests

5.22 Doctors in California are subject to the standards set forth by the:

(a) AAP

(b) ACA

(c) MPA

(d) MTA

5.23 You discover that a patient has hepatitis B. The patient does not want to tell his girlfriend because he is afraid she will leave him. You should:

(a) call the police

(b) tell his girlfriend because she has a right to know

(c) tell his parents

(d) tell no one

Answers on page 91

5.24 Informed consent means:

(a) A patient's medical records are available for healthcare workers to review

(b) a doctor explains test results to the patient

(c) the patient agrees to a procedure after being told the consequences associated with it

(d) the patient has the right to see their medical records and test results

5.25 California law under 22 CCR §72543 states that patient records should be kept for a minimum of how many years?

(a) 5

(b) 6

(c) 7

(d) 8

5.26 A law that restricts the period of time during which an action may be brought against another party is known as:

(a) common law

(b) litigation

(c) statute of limitations

(d) summons

Answers on page 91

5.27 Common law is also known as:

(a) case law

(b) private law

(c) public law

(d) universal law

5.28 California State law H&SC 118286 makes it illegal to dispose of which type of waste in the trash?

(a) Adult diapers

(b) Home-generated sharps

(c) Medical waste

(d) Unused medications

5.29 In which of these circumstances can a child's medical records be released?

(a) A lawyer needs the forms for a trial the next day

(b) A parent with legal custody signs the release forms

(c) The child gives verbal permission to release the records

(d) The child signs the release forms

5.30 Under which ethical principle do phlebotomists have a duty to obtain consent from patients before drawing blood?

(a) Beneficence

(b) Justice

(c) Nonmaleficence

(d) Respect for autonomy

Answers on page 91

5.31 Who enforces HIPAA?

(a) The Attorney General

(b) The Department of Health and Human Services

(c) The Surgeon General

(d) The US Senate

5.32 What does data privacy legislation deal with?

(a) The collection, use, and disclosure of personal information

(b) The control of private health care

(c) The privacy of health care workers

(d) The privatization of provincial health care

5.33 A phlebotomist collects blood from a 14-year-old girl without obtaining consent from her parents. The phlebotomist could be charged with:

(a) assault and battery

(b) invasion of privacy

(c) statute of limitations

(d) vicarious liability

Answers on page 91

5.34 Under the California Business and Professions Code, "patient abandonment" is defined as terminating patient care without written notice that treatment will be discontinued, and without:

(a) ensuring the patient has enough medication for the next 30 days

(b) giving at least 30 days' notice

(c) giving the patient ample time to find another doctor

(d) sending the patient's records to the new doctor

5.35 HIPAA stands for:

(a) Health Informatics Privacy and Administration Act

(b) Health Insurance Portability and Accountability Act

(c) Healthcare Industry Privacy and Accountability Act

(d) Hospital Income Public Administration Act

5.36 Under which ethical principle do lab assistants and technicians have a duty to protect confidential patient information?

(a) Beneficence

(b) Justice

(c) Nonmaleficence

(d) Respect for autonomy

Answers on page 92

5.37 A patient's right to know of and exercise control over his or her personal information is called:

(a) accountability

(b) confidentiality

(c) privacy

(d) security

5.38 The Affordable Care Act is also known as:

(a) Medicaid

(b) Medicare

(c) Medicare Advantage

(d) Obamacare

5.39 The California Sharps and Drug Takeback Bill requires manufacturers:

(a) to offer safe disposal methods for their products

(b) to refund consumers for faulty sharps and drug products

(c) to take back faulty sharps and drug products

(d) to take full responsibility for products disposed of irresponsibly

5.40 A patient rolls up his sleeve for a blood draw. Which type of consent is this?

(a) Active consent

(b) Explicit consent

(c) Implied consent

(d) Informed consent

Answers on page 92

5.41 According to the California Health and Safety Code, a practitioner may dispense a controlled substance classified in Schedule II directly to a user in an amount not to exceed a ____ hours supply.

(a) 24

(b) 48

(c) 72

(d) 96

5.42 A document that requires you to attend court and bring documents with you is called a:

(a) affidavit

(b) search warrant

(c) subpoena duces tecum

(d) summons

5.43 In California, laboratories must report a case of malaria to the local health officer within one:

(a) hour

(b) working day

(c) week

(d) month

Answers on page 92

5.44 __________ is the obligation of a person or organization to not disclose health information unless authorized by law or the person.

(a) Accountability

(b) Confidentiality

(c) Privacy

(d) Security

5.45 The obligation of a person or organization to preserve privacy by not disclosing or giving access to health information is called:

(a) access protection

(b) confidentiality

(c) privacy

(d) security

5.46 What is drug diversion?

(a) Moving excess boxes and vials of medication into off-site, long-term storage

(b) Switching a patient from a brand-name medication to a generic medication

(c) The deflection of prescription medications into the illegal market

(d) When a patient weans off an addictive medication

5.47 Living wills concern which of the following?

(a) Division of assets

(b) Funeral costs

(c) Medical treatment

(d) Taxes

Answers on page 92

5.48 Which of these is not a requirement for a living will?

(a) At least two adults must witness the declarant signing the will

(b) The declarant must be of sound mind

(c) The declarant must have an uncurable illness

(d) The will must be made in writing

5.49 Which act requires health care agencies to inform patients with Medicare about advance directives?

(a) Affordable Care Act

(b) Health Insurance Portability and Accountability Act

(c) Patient Safety and Quality Improvement Act

(d) Patient Self Determination Act

5.50 In California, what color are biohazard bags for medical waste?

(a) Orange

(b) Red

(c) Yellow

(d) Black

5.51 California living will law is encoded in which act?

(a) Final Wishes Act

(b) Natural Death Act

(c) Right to Civil Death Act

(d) Right to Peaceful Death Act

Answers on page 92

5.52 Which act prevents employers from retaliatiing againist workers for complaining about unsafe working conditions?

(a) Fair Labor Standards Act

(b) Federal Employees' Compensation Act

(c) Occupational Safety & Health Act

(d) Uniformed Services Employment and Reemployment Rights Act

5.53 California Senate Bill 41 (SB41) is an HIV prevention that allows pharmacists to sell how many syringes to a person without a prescription?

(a) 10

(b) 15

(c) 25

(d) 30

5.54 In California, laboratories must report a case of smallpox to the local health officer within one:

(a) hour

(b) working day

(c) week

(d) month

Answers on page 93

5.55 What is meant by a chain of custody?

(a) Chains used to restrain a prisoner during phlebotomy

(b) The management hierarchy in a hospital

(c) The process of documenting the handling of evidence

(d) The sequence of parents and/or caregivers in a child's life

5.56 What is the Lanterman–Petris–Short Act?

(a) An act that protects the privacy of people who undergo blood testing for HIV

(b) An act that provides universal health care to Californians

(c) An act that regulates involuntary commitment to mental health institutions

(d) An act that requires healthcare providers to give a free copy of medical records to patients

5.57 Medical malpractice requires four elements to be met for the plaintiff to recover damages. One of these elements is:

(a) do no harm

(b) duty of care

(c) ethical dilemma

(d) justice

Answers on page 93

5.58 A legal document that specifies the nature and level of treatment that a person wants to receive in the event of later being unable to make those decisions is a(n):

(a) advance directive

(b) alternate level of care directive

(c) delegated act

(d) end of life directive

5.59 What is the age of consent in California for the treatment of sexually transmitted diseases?

(a) 12

(b) 13

(c) 14

(d) 15

5.60 A patient is terminally ill and lacks the capacity to make her own health care decisions. Her living will states that she does not want life-prolonging procedures and she wants to die a natural death. Her physician says she needs a nasogastric tube, which will give her three months more to live. The patient's surrogate decision-maker does not want the tube inserted. Californian law requires the hospital to:

(a) find a new surrogate decision-maker

(b) insert the tube

(c) not insert the tube and let the patient die

(d) wait seven days to make a decision

Answers on page 93

5.61 A nurse misidentifies a patient and gives the patient the wrong medication. As a result, the patient is seriously injured. What type of crime did the nurse commit?

(a) Assault

(b) Battery

(c) Misdemeanour

(d) Negligence

5.62 The words "11159.2 exemption" on a prescription in California indicate that a patient is:

(a) HIV-positive

(b) incarcerated

(c) terminally ill

(d) unable to make their own healthcare decisions

5.63 A(n) ________________ is a legal document in which a person specifies what actions should be taken for their health if they are no longer able to make decisions for themselves.

(a) Cy-près doctrine

(b) advance directive

(c) blind trust

(d) determination policy

Answers on page 93

5.64 Who does the Good Samaritan Act protect?

(a) Doctors performing euthanasia

(b) Patients giving gifts to doctors

(c) People giving first aid

(d) People who find lost property

5.65 On which ethical principle is informed consent based?

(a) Autonomy

(b) Beneficence

(c) Fidelity

(d) Veracity

5.66 Which Californian law makes it illegal for employers to fire employees for discriminatory reasons?

(a) BCCA

(b) CCPA

(c) CTSCA

(d) FEHA

5.67 Which of these complaints would the California medical board not investigate?

(a) Inappropriate prescribing

(b) Sexual misconduct

(c) Cases of unlicensed practice

(d) Billing disputes

Answers on page 94

5.68 A patient asks a lab assistant for test results. What should the lab assistant do?

(a) Call the patient at home

(b) Give the results to the patient

(c) Let the patient check her results on the lab computer

(d) Refer the request to the supervisor

5.69 Which of these applies to HIPAA requirements?

(a) Healthcare facilities must inform patients, in writing, about the disclosure of identifiable health information

(b) Patients should be informed of available resources for resolving disputes

(c) Patients should know the identity of people involved in their care

(d) Patients should know the long-term costs of treatment choices

5.70 The End of Life Option Act allows terminally ill patients expected to die within six months to end their lives with the assistance of a:

(a) insurer

(b) lawyer

(c) physician

(d) spouse

Answers on page 94

5.71 In California, the maximum punishment for illegally prescribing a controlled substance is up to ___ year(s) imprisonment and a fine of up to ________.

(a) 1, $20,000

(b) 2, $40,000

(c) 3, $60,000

(d) 4, $80,000

5.72 What does the term "standard of care" mean?

(a) All the doctors, nurses and other professionals who play a role in a patient's care

(b) The legal standards a healthcare facility must meet

(c) The reasonable degree of care a clinician should provide to a patient

(d) Who has the right to access a patient's personal health information

Answers on page 94

Answers for Section 5: Legal and Ethical Issues

5.1 **d) Security**

5.2 **b) working day**
Acute HIV infections must be reported both by telephone and to the state electronic reporting system within one working day of identification.

5.3 **d) an invasion of privacy**

5.4 **d) protected**
PHI is an acronym of Protected Health Information. The term is commonly referred to in the Health Insurance Portability and Accountability Act (HIPAA).

5.5 **c) informed consent**

5.6 **b) Confidentiality**

5.7 **a) common law**

5.8 **b) A public health occurrence**

5.9 **c) Medical power of attorney**

5.10 **b) negligence**

5.11 **a) accountability**

5.12 **a) say nothing to his girlfriend**

5.13 **b) When the pharmacy is in the hospital where the unlicensed person works**
Article 1 of the California Code Health and Safety Code says, "A prescription written by an unlicensed person lawfully practicing medicine pursuant to Section 2065 of the Business and Professions Code, shall be filled only at a pharmacy maintained in the hospital which employs such unlicensed person."

5.14 **d) workers can quit or be fired for any reason, as long as the reason is not illegal**

5.15 **b) 2**

5.16 **a) Contract law**
Contract law is an area of law that enforces legally binding agreements.

5.17 **c) Yes, until 15 days before the hearing**

5.18 **b) consent**

5.19 **d) Verifying the phone number of the receiving location before faxing confidential material**

5.20 **d) must never be discussed outside the hospital**

5.21 **d) Tell the lawyer that the laboratory can only release information to the physician who ordered the tests**

5.22 **c) MPA**

Doctors in California are subject to the standards set forth in the Medical Practice Act (MPA), which is set forth in the Business and Professions Code.

5.23 **d) tell no one**

In this situation, the patient's right to confidentiality takes precedence. Hopefully, the patient would discuss the results with his partner but it is not for a lab professional to decide.

5.24 **c) the patient agrees to a procedure after being told the consequences associated with it**

5.25 **c) 7**

22 CCR §72543 states, "All health records of discharged patients shall be completed and filed within 30 days after discharge date and such records shall be kept for a minimum of 7 years."

5.26 **c) statute of limitations**

5.27 **a) case law**

Common law is also known as case law.

5.28 **b) Home-generated sharps**

5.29 **b) A parent with legal custody signs the release forms**

5.30 **d) Respect for autonomy**

5.31 **b) The Department of Health and Human Services**

The primary enforcer of HIPAA is the Office for Civil Rights of the Department of Health and Human Services.

5.32 **a) The collection, use, and disclosure of personal information**

Data privacy laws provide a legal framework on how to obtain, use, store, and disclose people's data.

5.33 **a) assault and battery**

5.34 **c) giving the patient ample time to find another doctor**

5.35 **b) Health Insurance Portability and Accountability Act**

5.36 **d) Respect for autonomy**

5.37 **c) privacy**

5.38 **d) Obamacare**

5.39 **a) to offer safe disposal methods for their products**

5.40 **c) Implied consent**
Implied consent is granted implicitly by the patient's actions rather than directly granted.

5.41 **c) 72**

5.42 **c) subpoena duces tecum**

5.43 **b) working day**

5.44 **b) Confidentiality**

5.45 **b) confidentiality**

5.46 **c) The deflection of prescription medications into the illegal market**

5.47 **c) Medical treatment**
A living will is a document expressing an individual's medical treatment preferences in the event they become unconscious or otherwise unable to communicate.

5.48 **c) The declarant must have an uncurable illness**

5.49 **d) Patient Self Determination Act**
The Patient Self Determination Act requires health care agencies receiving funds through Medicaid or Medicare to provide information about advance directives to their patients.

5.50 **b) Red**
Red biohazard bags must be used for medical waste, which is regulated by the California Department of Health Services (DHS)

5.51 **b) Natural Death Act**

5.52 **c) Occupational Safety & Health Act**

5.53 **d) 30**
California Senate Bill 41 (SB41), effective January 2012, is designed to expand syringe access among injection drug users by allowing pharmacists to sell up to 30 syringes without a prescription.

5.54 **a) hour**

5.55 **c) The process of documenting the handling of evidence**

Chain of custody is the process of maintaining a record of all the people who come into contact with a specimen before a test is complete. The specimen is packaged in a permanently sealed, tamper-proof container. A chain of custody form is required; the form accompanies the specimen throughout the testing process and is used to document the identity of anyone who handles the specimen.

5.56 **c) An act that regulates involuntary commitment to mental health institutions**

The Lanterman–Petris–Short Act regulates involuntary civil commitment to a mental health institution in the state of California.

5.57 **b) duty of care**

The four elements of medical malpractice are duty of care, breach of duty, harm, and causation.

5.58 **a) advance directive**

5.59 **a) 12**

Under California law, minors aged 12 years or older may consent to medical care for the diagnosis, treatment and prevention of sexually transmitted diseases.

5.60 **c) not insert the tube and let the patient die**

5.61 **d) Negligence**

5.62 **c) terminally ill**

A prescription with the words "11159.2 exemption" means the patient is terminally ill.

5.63 **b) advance directive**

5.64 **c) People giving first aid**

5.65 **a) Autonomy**

Informed consent is based on a patient's right to make decisions about his or her own health care, with adequate information to make that decision.

5.66 **d) FEHA**

The California Fair Employment and Housing Act (FEHA) makes it illegal for employers to fire at-will employees for discriminatory reasons such as race, religion, age, and gender.

The BCCA is the Buy Clean California Act.

The CCPA is the California Consumer Privacy Act and is intended to enhance privacy rights and consumer protection.

The CTSCA is the California Transparency in Supply Chain Act.

5.67 **d) Billing disputes**

5.68 **d) Refer the request to the supervisor**

5.69 **a) Healthcare facilities must inform patients, in writing, about the disclosure of identifiable health information**

The Health Insurance Portability and Accountability Act (HIPAA) is a federal law that protects sensitive patient health information from being disclosed without the patient's consent or knowledge.

5.70 **c) physician**

The End of Life Option Act is a California law that allows certain terminally ill adults to request a prescription for an aid-in-dying drug. The assistance of a physician is required.

5.71 **a) 1, $20,000**

Under California Health and Safety Code 11153(b), you can face up to a year in jail and a fine of up to $20,000 for writing illegal prescriptions for controlled drugs.

5.72 **c) The reasonable degree of care a clinician should provide to a patient**

In a medical setting, the standard of care is the degree of care and skill that the average health care provider would be expected to deliver when caring for patients.

Section 6
Patient Education

There are 75 questions in this section.

6.1 A medication indicated as PRN should be taken:

(a) by mouth

(b) once a day

(c) rectally

(d) when needed

6.2 Which of these fibers is insoluble?

(a) Cellulose

(b) Mucilage

(c) Psyllium

(d) Wheat dextrin

Answers on page 116

6.3 A patient with GERD should avoid which of these foods?

(a) Chocolate

(b) Egg whites

(c) Ginger

(d) Oatmeal

6.4 Which instruction would be beneficial to include in nutritional therapy for patients with hypertension?

(a) Eliminate foods that contain lactose from the diet

(b) Increase the percentage of calories from saturated fats to 30%

(c) Restrict potassium intake by limiting the intake of fruits and vegetables

(d) Restrict sodium intake to 2 to 3 g per day

6.5 Patches, ointments, creams, liquids and sprays are given via which route of drug administration?

(a) Otic

(b) Sublingual

(c) Topical

(d) Urethral

6.6 What is the pharmacy abbreviation for "once per day"?

(a) q.d.

(b) q.h.

(c) q.i.d.

(d) q.o.d.

Answers on page 116

6.7 A lack or shortage of a vitamin or mineral is called a:

(a) anemia

(b) deficiency

(c) scarcity

(d) toxicity

6.8 A patient needs to eat 25 grams of fiber per day. If she starts the day with two 2 pieces of toast, and each piece of toast contains 2.2 g of fiber, then how many grams of fiber does she still need to eat that day?

(a) 20.6 grams

(b) 22.2 grams

(c) 23.8 grams

(d) 24.2 grams

6.9 What is the pharmacy abbreviation for the right ear?

(a) AD

(b) AS

(c) ASA

(d) AU

Answers on page 116

6.10 Which of these written instructions would be easiest for a patient to understand?

(a) Monitor temperature every four hours and notify the provider if over 38

(b) Monitor temperature every four hours and notify the provider if over 38°C

(c) Monitor temperature q4 and notify the provider if over 38

(d) Monitor temperature q4 and notify the provider if over 38°C

6.11 Which of these foods is a good source of vitamin E?

(a) Citrus fruits

(b) Lean meats

(c) Milk and dairy products

(d) Vegetable oils

6.12 What is the difference between vitamins and minerals?

(a) Vitamins are always needed in larger amounts than minerals

(b) Vitamins are essential whereas nutrients are not essential

(c) Vitamins are organic whereas minerals are inorganic

(d) Vitamins provide energy whereas minerals help the body to use energy

6.13 Which of these is colloquially known as bad cholesterol?

(a) Fat

(b) HDL

(c) LDL

(d) Triglyceride

Answers on page 117

6.14 A patient has a prescription that says "1 tab PO qd". What does this mean?

(a) Take 1 tablet after meals and 1 tablet at bedtime

(b) Take 1 tablet every day by mouth

(c) Take 1 tablet four times a day with meals

(d) Take 1 tablet rectally at bedtime

6.15 What does the pharmaceutical abbreviation "pc" mean?

(a) After meals

(b) At bedtime

(c) Before meals

(d) In the morning

6.16 Food labels list ingredients in which order?

(a) Alphabetical order

(b) By the manufacturer's order of preference

(c) Descending order by weight

(d) The most harmful ingredients first

6.17 The patient requires 600 mg of Tagamet but only 300 mg tablets are available. How many tablets should the patient take?

(a) 1

(b) 2

(c) 3

(d) 4

Answers on page 117

6.18 What is annotation?

(a) Adding notes to a text

(b) Assessing the normal and abnormal values in lab tests

(c) Converting speech to a written document

(d) Proofreading a written document

6.19 To establish an EER for a patient, you need to know their age, gender, weight, height, and:

(a) bone mineral density

(b) heart rate

(c) income

(d) level of physical activity

6.20 Basic metabolic rate accounts for approximately ________ of total daily energy expenditure in individuals with a sedentary occupation.

(a) 20–35%

(b) 40–55%

(c) 60–75%

(d) 80–95%

Answers on page 117

6.21 Which of these may change a patient's nutritional status and needs?

(a) Drugs

(b) Fruits

(c) Poultry

(d) Starch

6.22 What is the recommended daily calorie intake for men?

(a) 1,500 calories

(b) 2,500 calories

(c) 3,500 calories

(d) 500 calories

6.23 Which of these is a kidney function test?

(a) BUN

(b) CBC

(c) HCT

(d) INR

6.24 What is the main carbohydrate in milk?

(a) Glycogen

(b) Lactose

(c) Starch

(d) Sucrose

Answers on page 118

6.25 A patient has a prescription that says "1 tab po qid pc & hs". What does this mean?

(a) For the first week, take one tablet by mouth every 6 hours as needed, and then take one tablet every 24 hours as needed

(b) Take one tablet by mouth four times a day, after meals and at bedtime

(c) Take one tablet by mouth two times a day, in the morning and at bedtime

(d) Take one tablet once per day for 14 days then one tablet once per day for 7 days

6.26 Which of these is a non-modifiable risk factor for heart disease?

(a) Age

(b) Obesity

(c) Physical inactivity

(d) Tobacco use

6.27 Which of these terms would patients most easily understand?

(a) Dilation

(b) Erythema

(c) Purpura

(d) Redness

Answers on page 118

6.28 Patients who eat little fiber, drink inadequate fluids, and have sedentary lifestyles are likely to experience which dietary symptom?

(a) Constipation

(b) Diarrhea

(c) Heartburn

(d) Vomiting

6.29 Which of the following is not one of the six classes of nutrients?

(a) Alcohol

(b) Minerals

(c) Vitamins

(d) Water

6.30 Which of these could cause high blood glucose levels in a diabetic patient?

(a) A low-carb diet

(b) Missed insulin injections

(c) Missed meals

(d) Too much insulin

6.31 White rice has a glycemic index of 70. What is the glycemic load of 50 g of white rice?

(a) 0.714

(b) 1.4

(c) 3,500

(d) 35

Answers on page 118

6.32 To provide protection against neural tube defects, when should a woman start taking folate?

(a) After the pregnancy has been confirmed

(b) At the start of the second trimester

(c) At the start of the third trimester

(d) At the time of conception

6.33 Urine samples for culture should be collected in:

(a) containers cleaned with disinfectant

(b) containers containing an anticoagulant

(c) narrow-mouthed containers

(d) sterile containers

6.34 What type of exercise is running?

(a) High impact

(b) Low impact

(c) Medium impact

(d) No impact

6.35 The acronym PPT stands for what blood test?

(a) Partial thrombin time

(b) Partial thromboplastin time

(c) Proportional thrombin time

(d) Proportional thromboplastin time

Answers on page 118

6.36 Which of these is an essential amino acid?

(a) Alanine

(b) Asparagine

(c) Lysine

(d) Serine

6.37 Blood glucose levels below normal levels is called:

(a) hyperglucosia

(b) hyperglycaemia

(c) hypoglucosia

(d) hypoglycaemia

6.38 Which of these foods can be eaten on a low-fat diet?

(a) Cake with icing

(b) Chicken with skin attached

(c) Skinless chicken breast

(d) Whole milk

6.39 If a food has a glycemic index of 90 and contains 50 g of carbohydrate, what is the glycaemic load?

(a) 45

(b) 50

(c) 90

(d) 140

Answers on page 119

6.40 The three major disaccharides are:

(a) glucose, galactose, and fructose

(b) glucose, lactose, and sucrose

(c) lactase, fructase, and galactase

(d) sucrose, lactose, and maltose

6.41 Which body tissue stores unneeded, extra energy?

(a) Bone

(b) Fat

(c) Muscle

(d) Skin

6.42 Which of these foods has the lowest glycemic index?

(a) Broccoli

(b) Meat

(c) Potatoes

(d) Rice

6.43 What does the pharmaceutical abbreviation "qid" mean?

(a) Every day

(b) Every hour

(c) Four days a week

(d) Four times a day

Answers on page 119

6.44 Which of these medications lowers the level of LDL cholesterol in the blood?

(a) Beta-blockers

(b) Corticosteroid

(c) Diuretics

(d) Statins

6.45 Which of these health problems is related to poor nutrition and lifestyle factors?

(a) Hemochromatosis

(b) Hypertension

(c) Lyme disease

(d) Thalassemia

6.46 Which of these foods is highest in folate?

(a) Green, leafy vegetables

(b) Meats

(c) Mlik

(d) Vegetable oil

6.47 Which of the following does not contain calories?

(a) Beer

(b) Soluble fiber

(c) Vodka

(d) Water

Answers on page 119

6.48 Diabetics should eat a diet low in:

(a) dairy products

(b) gluten

(c) salt

(d) sugar

6.49 Night blindness is caused by a deficiency in which vitamin?

(a) Vitamin A

(b) Vitamin B12

(c) Vitamin B6

(d) Vitamin C

6.50 Which of these foods should a lactose-intolerant patient avoid?

(a) Apples

(b) Feta

(c) Potatoes

(d) Rice

6.51 What does the acronym FITT stand for?

(a) Fitness, intensity, time, and type

(b) Fitness, intensity, total, and type

(c) Frequency, intensity, time, and type

(d) Frequency, intensity, total, and type

Answers on page 120

6.52 Identify the false statement regarding 24-hour urine collection.

(a) A preservative may be used for some tests

(b) Collections during the night are discarded

(c) Testing is done in clinical chemistry

(d) The first timed specimen is discarded

6.53 Which of these is included in a complete blood count?

(a) Cholesterol levels

(b) Erythrocyte sedimentation rate

(c) Hematocrit

(d) pH

6.54 Which of the following lipids is an essential nutrient?

(a) Cholesterol

(b) Lecithin

(c) Linoleic acid

(d) Stearic acid

6.55 Which route of drug administration involves placing the drug into the ear via drops?

(a) Buccal

(b) Otic

(c) Parenteral

(d) Sublingual

Answers on page 120

6.56 Which of these actions should a diabetic patient take if they are experiencing hypoglycemia?

(a) Check their urine for ketones

(b) Eat something sugary

(c) Inject themselves with insulin

(d) Run on the spot

6.57 Which of these statements about carbohydrate loading is true?

(a) It is a strategy used by diabetics

(b) It is key for weight loss activities

(c) It is recommended for anyone exercising

(d) It is used to build glycogen stores

6.58 If a patient eats a meal containing 70 g of carbohydrate and their insulin to carbohydrate ratio is 1 unit of bolus insulin for every 10 g of carbohydrate, then how many units of bolus insulin would they need to take?

(a) 1 unit

(b) 7 units

(c) 10 units

(d) 70 units

Answers on page 120

6.59 In which disease is the body unable to use glucose for energy?

(a) Diabetes

(b) Diverticulosis

(c) Hypoglycemia

(d) Stroke

6.60 What is the body mass index of a man who is 180 cm tall and weighs 82 kg?

(a) 22.1

(b) 23.8

(c) 24.2

(d) 25.3

6.61 Medical assistants can teach patients about the role of nutrition in helping prevent specific

(a) Healthy diets

(b) Medical conditions

(c) Medical cures

(d) Point systems

6.62 Patients with heart disease should lower their intake of:

(a) fish

(b) fruit

(c) potassium

(d) salt

Answers on page 120

6.63 Which of these cholesterol results is consistent with increased risk for cardiovascular disease?

(a) Low HDL and high LDL

(b) Low LDL and high HDL

(c) Low VLDL and high HDL

(d) Low chylomicrons and high HDL

6.64 Which urine collection technique involves collecting the urine by inserting a sterile needle into the patient's bladder through the abdominal wall?

(a) Biopsy

(b) Necropsy

(c) Suprapubic aspiration

(d) Urinary catheter

6.65 Which of these foods is high in omega-3 fatty acids?

(a) Beef

(b) Chicken

(c) Fish

(d) Lamb

Answers on page 121

6.66 Which vitamin do pregnant women take to help prevent neural tube defects in the fetus?

(a) Biotin

(b) Folic acid

(c) Niacin

(d) Pantothenic acid

6.67 What is the recommended daily calorie intake for women?

(a) 1,000 calories

(b) 2,000 calories

(c) 3,000 calories

(d) 4,000 calories

6.68 Which of the following is low in sodium?

(a) Bacon

(b) Bread

(c) Cheese

(d) Milk

6.69 A 750ml bottle of red wine is18% alcohol. How much alcohol does the bottle contain?

(a) 95 mL

(b) 135 mL

(c) 175 mL

(d) 215 mL

Answers on page 121

6.70 Which lipoprotein is the smallest?

(a) Chylomicron

(b) High-density lipoprotein

(c) Low-density lipoprotein

(d) Very-low-density lipoprotein

6.71 Which of these foods contains no sugar?

(a) Milk

(b) Nuts

(c) Olive oil

(d) Seeds

6.72 What supplement would a patient with osteoporosis need?

(a) Calcium

(b) Iron

(c) Thiamine

(d) Vitamin K

6.73 What type of exercise produces the most stress on the joints?

(a) High impact

(b) Low impact

(c) Medium impact

(d) No impact

Answers on page 121

6.74 What is the pharmacy abbreviation for "by mouth"?

(a) ou

(b) po

(c) pr

(d) pv

6.75 Clean-catch urine specimens are necessary when testing urine for:

(a) bacteria

(b) glucose

(c) occult blood

(d) protein

Answers on page 121

Answers for Section 6: Patient Education

6.1 **d) when needed**

PRN is an acronym for "pro re nata" which means "as needed".

6.2 **a) Cellulose**

Cellulose is insoluble in water.

6.3 **a) Chocolate**

Patients with GERD (gastroesophageal reflux disease) should avoid foods such as chocolate, alcohol, caffeine, and carbonated beverages because these foods can increase their symptoms.

6.4 **d) Restrict sodium intake to 2 to 3 g per day**

6.5 **c) Topical**

Topical drugs are drugs used on the skin, such as patches, ointments, and creams.

6.6 **a) q.d.**

q.d. (from the Latin "quaque die") means once per day.

q.h. means once every hour.

q.i.d. ("quater in die") means four times a day.

q.o.d. means every other day.

6.7 **b) deficiency**

6.8 **a) 20.6 grams**

$25 - (2 \times 2.2) = 20.6$

6.9 **a) AD**

AD is derived from Latin "auris dextra" and means "right ear".

AS means left ear.

ASA means aspirin.

AU means both ears.

6.10 **b) Monitor temperature every four hours and notify the provider if over 38°C**

Medical abbreviations, such as q4, should be avoided in written patient instructions Temperatures should be written with units, such as Celcius or Fahrenheit, to avoid confusion.

6.11 **d) Vegetable oils**

Good sources of vitamin E include vegetable oil, sunflower oil, olive oil. nuts and seeds. Lean meats, citrus fruits, and dairy products are generally low in vitamin E.

6.12 **c) Vitamins are organic whereas minerals are inorganic**

6.13 **c) LDL**

LDL (low-density lipoprotein) cholesterol is often called the "bad" cholesterol because it collects in the walls of the blood vessels.

6.14 **b) Take 1 tablet every day by mouth**

PO means orally and qd means once per day.

6.15 **a) After meals**

pc (post cibum) means "after meals".

6.16 **c) Descending order by weight**

On food labels, the ingredients are listed by the greatest amount first, followed in descending order by those in smaller amounts.

6.17 **b) 2**

300 mg $\times$ 2 = 600 mg

6.18 **a) Adding notes to a text**

6.19 **d) level of physical activity**

Estimated Energy Requirement (EER) is the average dietary energy intake that is predicted to maintain energy balance in healthy, normal-weight individuals of a defined age, gender, weight, height, and level of physical activity.

6.20 **c) 60–75%**

6.21 **a) Drugs**

6.22 **b) 2,500 calories**

6.23 **a) BUN**

The BUN (blood urea nitrogen) test measures the amount of urea nitrogen in the blood, which reveals how well the kidneys are working.

A CBC is a complete blood count.

HCT (hematocrit) indicates the volume of red blood cells in the blood.

The INR (international normalized ratio) is a measurement of how long it takes blood to form a clot.

6.24 **b) Lactose**

Lactose is the main carbohydrate in milk. It is a simple carbohydrate that makes up around 5% of milk.

6.25 **b) Take one tablet by mouth four times a day, after meals and at bedtime**

po = by mouth
qid = four times a day
pc = after meals
hs = at bedtime

6.26 **a) Age**

A non-modifiable risk factor is a factor that cannot be changed. Age is such a factor because patients cannot change their age. Other non-modifiable risk factors for heart disease are ethnic background and a family history of heart disease.

Physical activity, obesity, tobacco use and diet are all modifiable risk factors because they can be changed.

6.27 **d) Redness**

Patients may not understand medical terms, so it is best to use everyday words where possible.

6.28 **a) Constipation**

6.29 **a) Alcohol**

The six classes of nutrients are carbohydrates, lipids, proteins, water, vitamins, and minerals. They are all needed by the body to function properly.

6.30 **b) Missed insulin injections**

If a diabetic patient misses insulin injections, their blood glucose levels will rise.

The other options all cause low blood glucose levels, not high blood glucose levels.

6.31 **d) 35**

Glycemic load = (amount of the food in grams $\times$ the food's glycemic index) /100
So, the glycemic load of white rice = $(50 \times 70) / 100 = 35$

6.32 **d) At the time of conception**

6.33 **d) sterile containers**

6.34 **a) High impact**

High impact exercises move both feet off the ground at the same time. Examples include jumping, burpees, running, and jumping jacks.

6.35 **b) Partial thromboplastin time**

6.36 **c) Lysine**

Lysine is an essential amino acid because the body cannot produce it.

Alanine, aspartic acid, asparagine, glutamic acid, and serine, are non-essential because the body can synthesize them in sufficient quantities.

6.37 **d) hypoglycaemia**

6.38 **c) Skinless chicken breast**

6.39 **a) 45**

Glycemic load = (amount of the food in grams $\times$ the food's glycemic index) /100
So, the glycemic load here = (50 $\times$90) / 100 = 45

6.40 **d) sucrose, lactose, and maltose**

6.41 **b) Fat**

The body changes excess energy into fat.

6.42 **b) Meat**

Meat has a glycemic index of zero because it contains no carbohydrates.

6.43 **d) Four times a day**

6.44 **d) Statins**

Statins are medicines that lower the level of low-density lipoprotein (LDL) cholesterol in the blood.

Beta-blockers slow down the heart by blocking the action of hormones like adrenaline.

Corticosteroids are an anti-inflammatory medicine.

Diuretics increase urine output.

6.45 **b) Hypertension**

Nutrition and lifestyle factors, such as being overweight and having an unhealthy diet, increase the risk of hypertension (high blood pressure).

Hemochromatosis is also an inherited disorder, caused by a faulty gene.

Lyme disease is caused by a bacteria.

Thalassemia is an inherited blood disorder.

6.46 **a) Green, leafy vegetables**

6.47 **d) Water**

6.48 **d) sugar**

Diabetes is a condition that causes a person's blood sugar level to become too high. Therefore, diabetics need to eat a diet low in sugar.

6.49 **a) Vitamin A**

6.50 **b) Feta**

6.51 **c) Frequency, intensity, time, and type**

FITT is an acronym that stands for Frequency, Intensity, Time, and Type. It is used to create exercise plans.

6.52 **b) Collections during the night are discarded**

6.53 **c) Hematocrit**

A complete blood count includes red blood cell count, white blood cell count, platelet count, hemoglobin, and hematocrit.

6.54 **c) Linoleic acid**

6.55 **b) Otic**

6.56 **b) Eat something sugary**

Hypoglycemia is a condition where blood glucose levels are lower than normal. It is often caused when diabetics inject themselves with too much insulin. The remedy is to eat 15 to 20 grams of fast-acting carbohydrates, such as candy, fruit juice, or glucose tablets.

6.57 **d) It is used to build glycogen stores**

6.58 **b) 7 units**

6.59 **a) Diabetes**

6.60 **d) 25.3**

Body mass index = weight in kg / height in meters ^{2}

Body mass index = $82/1.8^2$

Body mass index = $82/3.24$

Body mass index = 25.3

6.61 **b) Medical conditions**

6.62 **d) salt**

Salt raises blood pressure, which can be dangerous for patients with heart disease.

Potassium lowers the risk of cardiovascular disease.

6.63 **a) Low HDL and high LDL**

LDL and VLDL are bad cholesterol. High levels of LDL increase the risk of heart disease.

HDL is good cholesterol. High levels of HDL decrease the risk of heart disease. Low levels would increase the risk of heart disease.

6.64 **c) Suprapubic aspiration**

Suprapubic aspiration is a procedure to take an uncontaminated urine sample to diagnose a urinary tract infection. It involves putting a needle through the skin just above the pubic bone into the bladder. It is typically used to collect urine in children who are not yet toilet trained.

6.65 **c) Fish**

6.66 **b) Folic acid**

Folic acid reduces the risk of neural tube defects in fetuses.

6.67 **b) 2,000 calories**

6.68 **d) Milk**

Milk has a small amount of naturally-occurring sodium.

Bread is relatively high in sodium. In fact, is the top contributor to dietary sodium in the US.

6.69 **b) 135 mL**

750 mL $\times$ 0.18 = 135 mL

6.70 **b) High-density lipoprotein**

6.71 **c) Olive oil**

Oils, such as olive oil and vegetable oil, contain no carbohydrates or sugar.

6.72 **a) Calcium**

People with osteoporosis are at high risk for broken bones. Calcium supplements can help to strengthen their bones.

6.73 **a) High impact**

6.74 **b) po**

ou means "each eye".

pr means rectally.

pv means vaginally.

6.75 **a) bacteria**

A clean-catch is a way of collecting urine without contaminating the urine sample with bacteria from the skin. This method is needed for urine culture tests, to prevent false positives.

Made in the USA
Middletown, DE
01 September 2023